A Note to P[arents]

DK READERS is a compelling program for beginning readers, designed in conjunction with leading literacy experts, including Dr. Linda Gambrell, Distinguished Professor of Education at Clemson University. Dr. Gambrell has served as President of the National Reading Conference, the College Reading Association, and the International Reading Association.

Beautiful illustrations and superb full-color photographs combine with engaging, easy-to-read stories to offer a fresh approach to each subject in the series. Each DK READER is guaranteed to capture a child's interest while developing his or her reading skills, general knowledge, and love of reading.

The five levels of DK READERS are aimed at different reading abilities, enabling you to choose the books that are exactly right for your child:

Pre-level 1: Learning to read
Level 1: Beginning to read
Level 2: Beginning to read alone
Level 3: Reading alone
Level 4: Proficient readers

The "normal" age at which a child begins to read can be anywhere from three to eight years old. Adult participation through the lower levels is very helpful for providing encouragement, discussing storylines, and sounding out unfamiliar words.

No matter which level you select, you can be sure that you are helping your child learn to read, then read to learn!

LONDON, NEW YORK, MUNICH,
MELBOURNE, AND DELHI

Series Editor Deborah Lock
U.S. Editor Shannon Beatty
Designer Neetika Vilash
Project Designer Akanksha Gupta
Art Director Martin Wilson
Production Editor Sarah Isle
Jacket Designer Natalie Godwin
Entomology Consultant Professor May
Berenbaum, University of Illinois
at Urbana-Champaign

Reading Consultant
Linda B. Gambrell, Ph.D.

First American Edition, 2012
12 13 14 15 16 10 9 8 7 6 5 4 3 2 1
001-184581-June 2012
Published in the United States by DK Publishing
375 Hudson Street, New York, New York 10014

DK books are available at special discounts when purchased in bulk for
sales promotions, premiums, fund-raising, or educational use.
For details, contact: DK Publishing Special Markets
375 Hudson Street, New York, New York 10014
SpecialSales@dk.com

A catalog record for this book is available
from the Library of Congress.

ISBN:978-0-7566-9278-0 (Paperback)
ISBN: 978-0-7566-9333-6 (Hardcover)

Color reproduction by Colourscan, Singapore
Printed and bound in China by L.Rex Printing Co., Ltd.
The publisher would like to thank the following for their kind
permission to reproduce their photographs:

(Key: a-above; b-below/bottom; c-center; f-far; l-left; r-right; t-top)

3 **Dreamstime.com:** Adina Chiriliuc (c). **Getty Images:** Andy
Roberts / OJO Images (ca). 4 **Getty Images:** James Porter / Workbook
Stock (t); Sabine Scheckel / Photodisc (c). 5 **Getty Images:** Don
Farrall / Stockbyte (b); James Porter / Workbook Stock (tr). 6-7
Corbis: Ron Wu / Monsoon / Photolibrary. 8 **Getty Images:** Philippe
Mercier / Workbook Stock (clb). 8-9 **Getty Images:** Konrad Wothe /
Minden Pictures. 9 **Getty Images:** Comstock / Comstock Images (t).
10 **Corbis:** Jonn / Johnér Images. **Photolibrary:** imagebroker (br). 11
Dreamstime.com: Andrzej Tokarski (t). **Getty Images:** Paul Tearle /
Stockbyte (bc). 12 **Getty Images:** Stephen Dalton / Minden Pictures.
13 **Getty Images:** Pal Teravagimov Photography / Flickr. 14-15 **Getty
Images:** Paulo De Oliveira / Oxford Scientific. 16-17 **Getty Images:**
Visuals Unlimited, Inc. / Alex Wild. 17 **Getty Images:** Konrad Wothe
/ Minden Pictures (t). 18-19 **Corbis:** Oswald Eckstein. 20 **Corbis:**
Darrell Gulin. 21 **Getty Images:** photoaraki.com / Flickr (t). 22
Corbis: Anthony Bannister / Gallo Images (t); Fritz Polking / Visuals
Unlimited. 23 **Corbis:** Stephanie Maze (t). 24 **Corbis:** James Hager /
Robert Harding World Imagery (t). 24-25 **Science Photo Library:** Dr
Morley Read. 26 **Photolibrary:** Garry DeLong (b). 27 **Corbis:** Ada
Summer (t). 28 **Getty Images:** Lew Robertson / FoodPix. 29 **Getty
Images:** Gavriel Jecan / Photodisc (t).

All other images © Dorling Kindersley
For further information see: www.dkimages.com

The publisher and author would also like to thank the
entomologists, Dr. Greg Zolnerowich, Gilbert Waldbauer
and Blake Newton for their advice.

Discover more at
www.dk.com

Contents

DK READERS

BEGINNING TO READ
1

Bugs and Us

Written by Patricia J. Murphy

DK Publishing

Buzz...

Buzz...

Buzz. Buzz.
Swat, swat!
Scratch. Scratch.
Splat, splat!
Insects can
really bug us!

Many buzz
in our ears.
Some bite or sting us.
Others can hurt our crops,
wreck our picnics—
and make people sick!

antenna

head

eye

thorax

You might ask,
"Who needs insects?"
The answer is,
"Everybody does!"

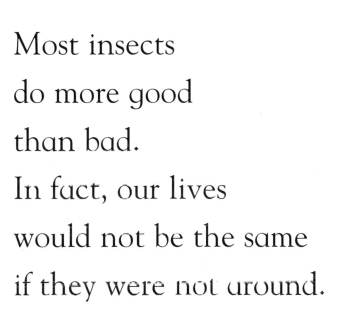

wing

Most insects
do more good
than bad.
In fact, our lives
would not be the same
if they were not around.

leg

abdomen

Bees, wasps, flies,
beetles, and butterflies
are great pollinators.
They buzz from flower to flower,
spreading pollen.
Pollen helps flowers make seeds.

pollen

Some of these seeds
grow into many of the fruits,
vegetables, and foods we eat.

Honey bees drink
nectar from flowers
and turn it
into honey.

nectar

They build honeycomb
with beeswax to store
both honey and pollen.
Many people and animals
love the taste of honey.
Beeswax is used
to make candles
and other things.

Some insects eat other insects!
This keeps insect groups
from getting too big.

A praying mantis eating a bee.

Dragonflies eat
300 to 400 mosquitoes a day.
Praying mantises and
green lacewings feast on
insects, large and small.
But, soon, other animal friends
will eat them!

A bee-eater
about to catch
a dragonfly.

Ladybugs and their larvae
are farmers' best friends.
They eat teeny
crop-eating insects
called aphids.

Ladybugs can't get
enough of them!
Many farmers use ladybugs
instead of sprays
that can harm
other living things.

larva

Some ants protect
plants from harm.
They bite and sting plant-eating
insects and other animals.
They act like bodyguards
for their plant pals.
Other ants move
seeds and soil around
so that new plants can grow.

Ants moving seeds.

Spiders help our gardens grow,
and keep our houses insect-free.
They catch and collect insects
in their wonderful webs.
These silky, sticky webs are
beautiful to look at.

Many insects are pretty
to watch—and to listen to.
Butterflies flash bright colors
and patterns as they flutter by.
Flickering fireflies
light up the night sky.
Chirping crickets sing
simple songs.

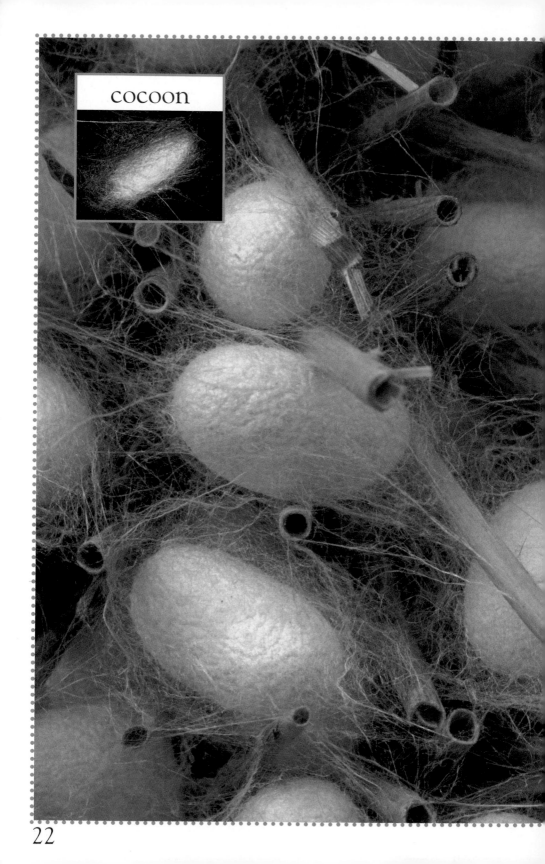

cocoon

Silkworm moths spin cocoons
with silky threads.
People collect these cocoons.
They weave the threads together
to make fine silk cloth.
It takes many cocoons
to make silky socks,
dresses, and shirts—
and lots of work, too.

Some insects do
nature's dirty work.
Dung beetles eat
the waste of animals.

Termites

Termites feed on rotting wood.
Flies and carrion beetles
feed on dead animals.
These insects rid the Earth
of waste—and help recycle it.

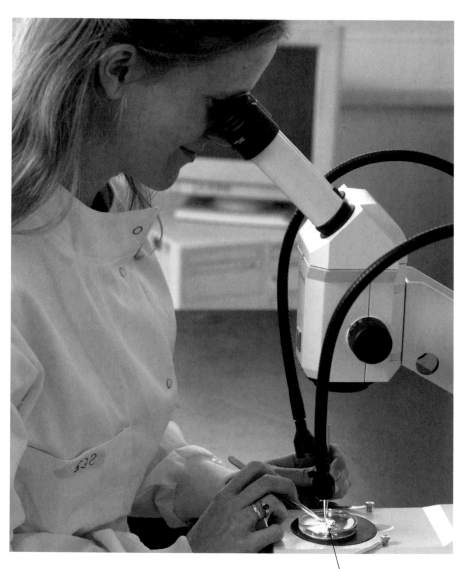

Other insects
help scientists.

Fruit flies and
flour beetles
show scientists how
animals change
as they grow.

medicine

Mayflies and stoneflies
tell them if streams are clean.
Beetles and butterflies help
them make new medicines
that could save people's lives.

Some insects are people's food.

In Africa, people eat
locusts and termites.

In Asia, people fry and roast
beetle larvae and bamboo worms.

These insects are tasty,
good for you—and there are
always plenty around!

Insects help us in many ways.
We can help them, too.
We can plant flowers
and grow plants.
We can learn
how to save their homes.
We can enjoy them—
and let them live.
Buzz.

Buzz.

Buzz.

Buzz.

Glossary

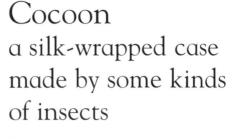

Cocoon
a silk-wrapped case made by some kinds of insects

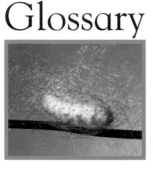

Larva
an insect during the early stage of its life

Medicine
a drug used to treat or prevent diseases

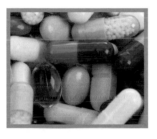

Nectar
the sugary sweet liquid from a flower

Pollen
a tiny grain that helps flowers make new seeds